Take time
to laugh.
♡JA.

If You Have to Ask . . .

Simple Answers to Life's Burning Questions

Mark Gonyea

RUNNING PRESS
PHILADELPHIA • LONDON

© 2010 by Mark Gonyea
All rights reserved under the Pan-American and International
Copyright Conventions
Printed in the United States

This book may not be reproduced in whole or in part, in any form or by any
means, electronic or mechanical, including photocopying, recording, or by any
information storage and retrieval system now known or hereafter invented,
without written permission from the publisher.

9   8   7   6   5   4   3   2   1
Digit on the right indicates the number of this printing

Library of Congress Control Number: 2009941702

ISBN 978-0-7624-3808-2
Cover and interior design by Mark Gonyea
Edited by Jennifer Leczkowski
Typography: Futura

Running Press Book Publishers
2300 Chestnut Street
Philadelphia, PA 19103-4371

Visit us on the web!
www.runningpress.com

I have that kind of face. You know the one I'm talking about, the kind that invites conversation from strangers. People just always seem willing to approach me with their questions; from the obvious ("Are we there yet?"), to the awkward ("Does this make me look fat?").

One day I started to ask my own questions: "Are there questions that answer themselves? Are there questions whose answers are *always* yes or *always* no?" Apparently there are, and quite a few in fact.

If You Have to Ask . . . is a collection of some of the very best, along with some illuminating commentary that will hopefully finally answer some of those universally annoying questions . . . so they will never need to be asked again!

Would you like a million dollars?

 YES NO

Are you just going to sit there in your underwear all day?

 YES   ☐ NO

Is it time to go home yet?

☐ YES ☑ NO

Not... Even... Close... Ask me again in another two minutes and I'll tell you the same thing. Now get back to work!

Do you want superpowers?

 YES ☐ NO

YES, YES, and YES! NOW! NOW! NOW! How cool would that be? WOOOSH! ZOOM! POW! I mean they're SUPER and they're POWERS, who wouldn't want them? No one, that's who!

Does this make me look fat?

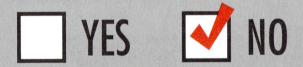

No. Period. End of story. Stop talking. Shut up. That's it. Game over. G'night folks. No. No. No. Now you might be tempted to try a "What, are you crazy?" DO NOT. I repeat, DO NOT. That only opens you up to a "Oh! So now I'm fat AND crazy!"

Seriously though, the answer is no.

Are we there yet?

☐ YES  NO

Is the car still moving? Good. Then we're obviously not there yet. When the car stops, get out. No, not now, we're still moving. No, this is a stop light. Look, I'll just tell you when to get out, ok? Good.

Oh yeah, absolutely! No way around it unfortunately (at least not yet). Sooner or later it happens to the best of us. Just try to look surprised. Oh, and if you could have a smile on your face when it happens, that'd be great. It makes people wonder what you were up to.

I'm disgusted! No one who could afford it would ever ask if they can. So put your coupons back in your pocket, sulk back to your basement apartment or where ever it was you crawled out from under and try to console yourself with copious amounts of cheap beer and basic cable. Actually, that doesn't sound so bad, wait for me!

Do you like my new haircut?

 YES   ☐ NO

It doesn't matter what it looks like, just say yes. Trust me, it'll save you a ton of hassle. There's really nothing she can do about it now anyway, she's stuck with the Darth Vader cut for at least three months.

May the force be with you.

Can I borrow your new _____ ?

☐ YES  NO

What? I just got it. Go get your own. Ok, maybe you can borrow it after I use it a few times. Geez, stop whining. I said after! Why don't you get a job instead of mooching everything off me? You know the rent is due this week, yeah, I thought that'd shut you up.

Can I punch you in the face?

☐ YES  NO

Granted, unlikely you'll be lucky enough to have someone ask before they punch you in the face. Your best bet will still be to say no, though chances are still very high you'll get punched. But maybe not in the face, at least.

Can I punch you in the face for a million dollars?

 YES ☐ NO

**Absolutely!
Thank you sir, may I have another?**

Something blah blah blah something blah something. Are you paying attention?

 YES  NO

We can still be friends, right?

☐ YES ☑ NO

Does this look infected to you?

☑ YES   ☐ NO

Gah! For the love of... Dude! Why would you show that to someone?

If it's gotten to the point where you need to ask if it's infected, it's infected.

Would you care to explain yourself?

☐ YES ☑ NO

Who me? What? Not really. Ummmm. You see, what happened was... wait... ok, let me start at the beginning. About a month ago, Steve, you know Steve from down in accounting, anyway. Steve and I had this ongoing bet... ok, wait. See, last night was... Bees! A huge swarm of bees came out of nowhere and...

Ok, the truth is, um, I tripped?

Can I interest you in a new long distance plan?

☐ YES ☑ NO

**Where did you get this number? I already told you no the last nine times you called! I swear if you don't take me off your damned call list right freaking now I'm going to come down there and strangle you with your own phone cord.
DO NOT TEST ME!**

Would you like fries with that?

✔ YES ☐ NO

I ordered a large number ten, didn't I? I'm pretty sure that implicitly means I want fries. And make sure they're hot, there's nothing worse than five-minute-old fries. And don't be dropping 'em and putting 'em back in the bin. Yeah, I'm watching you buddy.

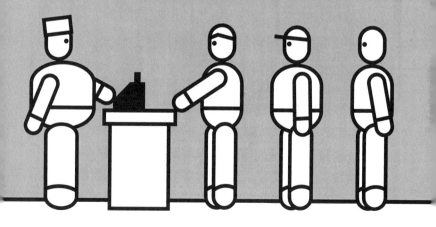

Braaaains?

☐ YES ☑ NO

No! Bad zombies! Hey, the guy next door has a really big 'ol juicy brain. I think he's a doctor. Yeah, ok, there you go. Bye bye now.

Do you like to role play?

 YES ☐ NO

Oh baby. Bring it on.

Do you like it now?

☐ YES ☑ NO

Um, now not so much, no.

Did I do something wrong, officer?

☑ YES ☐ NO

Please step out of the car, ma'am.

I bet you didn't see that coming?

☐ YES  NO

Oh really? You don't think I saw it coming, do you? You don't think I saw what was coming and dove in front of it on purpose so I could experience pain the likes of which I've never felt before and pray I never feel again. Is that what you don't think I did?

Was it good for you?

☑ YES   ☐ NO

Good? Hey. It was better than good, it was. . . um. . . really good? No, really. Of course I mean it. Oh, um. . . right now? Uh, hey, I just remembered I gotta get up kinda early tomorrow, so. . . I'll see ya. NO! Don't get up, that's ok, I'll let myself out.

Are you sure this is legal?

☐ YES  NO

Well, now's a heck of a time to start asking questions.

Hot enough for ya?

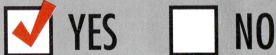 YES   ☐ NO

Why, can you make it hotter? I had no idea you were such good friends with Mother Nature. Now go away, you're blocking my sun.

Am I cool?

 YES  NO

Oh boy. Are you cool? ARE YOU COOL?
Dude! You are so not cool you're almost. . .
well, cool. But seriously, no, not cool.

Don't I know you?

☐ YES ☑ NO

Who me? Nope. You must be thinking of someone else. In fact, I wasn't even there. Where what? Oh geez, look at the time! Well, nice to meet you for the first time ever. Gotta go.

Should I hit a 12 when the dealer is showing a 7?

 YES  NO

Yeah, it's pretty much your only chance. If the dealer's down card is a 10 or better, you lose. If it's a 9 and the dealer draws a 5 or less, you lose. If you take a card and it's a 10 or more you lose. If... look, you're probably going to lose anyway so why don't you go try your luck at something with a little less math. Slots are fun. Lots of bright colors and shiny things. You like pushing buttons, right?

"I love treason but hate a traitor."

-Julius Caesar

You talkin' to me?

☑ YES   ☐ NO

You *talkin'* to me? You talkin' *to* me? You talkin' to *me*? Well, who the hell else are you talkin' to? *You* talkin' to me? Well, I'm the only one here.

What's the matter, don't you trust me?

☐ YES ✔ NO

Key elements of an untrustworthy person are the following: 1. Horns. People with horns are evil and are definitely not to be entered into contracts with. 2. Pointy tail. See previous. 3. Carries a pitchfork. Only two kinds of people carry pitchforks, farmers and people you shouldn't trust.

Are you going to eat that?

 YES  NO

Now you may or may not be eating that but why give it up without even trying. If they want to give you the option, take it.

Especially if it's pizza!

Is it that noticeable?

☐ YES ☑ NO

Aaaaaggghhhhh!!!
I mean, is *what* that noticeable?

Is everything you say a lie?

☑ YES ☐ NO

If everything you say is a lie, then that's a lie. But if that's a lie, then you're telling the truth... but you can't... because everything you say is a lie... but... truth... but... Danger! Danger! Does not compute! Does not compute! KA-BOOM!

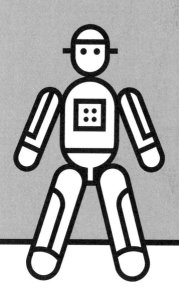

Have you been drinking?

☐ YES ✓ NO

No, but you really need to see this!
No, how do you go to the toilet?
No, I lost my car keys.
No, sometimes I just need a break.
No, I. . . blaaaarrrggh!

Are you ready to rock? I said, ARE YOU READY TO ROCK?

 YES  NO

Are you ok?

☐ YES ☑ NO

AAAAAA!!! No, I'm not OK! I have a pipe through my head!!! Do I look ok? Yeah, didn't think so. Now why don't you do something useful like call an ambulance. Then help me look for my eye because I HAVE A PIPE THROUGH MY HEAD!!!

Does this smell bad to you?

☑ YES ☐ NO

@#$%&*! (Gag) What died in there?
For the love of God open a window!
GAH! Why would you do that to me?
I think I need to lay down now.

You guys aren't from around here are you?

 YES  NO

Gleeb nork dag fweeble nada twip.

Translation: "This one will do.
Go set up the barbecue."

Can I get out of the box now?

☐ YES ☑ NO

Not until you learn.

You call that art?

 YES ☐ NO

 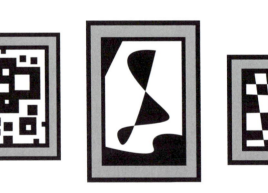 

Hmmm, let's see, canvas, check. Frame, check. Paint, check. Four years of art school, check. I don't know but it sure seems like art to me.

Are you going to get that?

☐ YES ✔ NO

RING! Obviously not. RING! If I was going to get it, I'd have gotten it by now, right? RING! I'm standing right here, there's no reason for me not to get it. RING! Unless I'm purposely choosing not to get for some unknown reason? RIN. . . There see, it stopped, problem solved.

Are those real?

 YES ☐ NO

As far as you'll ever know they are.

Do you want to know a secret?

☑ YES   ☐ NO

Psst psst pssst psssst pssst psst.

Ooooooo, no way!

Can't you keep a secret?

☐ YES NO

Of course not. What's the point of knowing a secret if you can't share it with a few friends. . . the cab driver. . . maybe one or two strangers in the supermarket and anyone that reads my blog or drives by the billboard on route 17. What?

Is it my turn?

 YES ☐ NO

Auuugh! YES! Here's a little hint, when you're sitting there staring at the tortured faces of all the other players waiting for someone to go, it's you.

Is this your card?

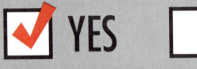 YES ☐ NO

Oooo, ahhhh, of course there's always a 1 in 52 chance of being right regardless. Does that really qualify as magic? At the very least, make something disappear! I volunteer my wife, HAH! Ahhh, I kid, I kid. I know you could never make anything disappear.

If a tree falls in the forest and no one is around to hear it, does it make a sound?

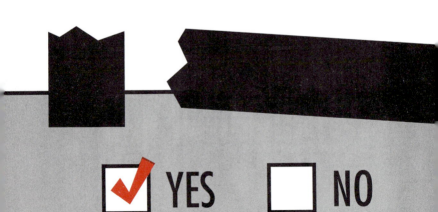

☑ YES ☐ NO

Does it make a sound, of course it does, it goes, "KERRRRRRR-RASH!" It doesn't matter if anyone was there to hear it. It still goes "KERRRRRR-RASH!"

Maybe someday we'll be chopping down trees in the vacuum of space, but till then. . . RUN LITTLE FOREST CREATURES! FALLING TREES!!! AAAAAA!!!! KERRRR-RASH!

Is there a problem with your dinner?

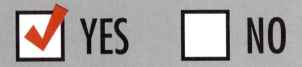 YES ☐ NO

Whatever gave you that idea?

Is this a good time?

 YES  NO

Actually, could you come back in about twenty minutes?

Mmmm, maybe thirty.

You know what, let's make it an hour.

Just take the rest of the day off.

Do you?

 YES ☐ NO

Um, well, I think, maybe. . .

"click."

Yes, I absolutely do! I do. I do. I do.

Are you happy now?

 YES ☐ NO

Oooooh, here it comes. You are soooo right. Bravo. Yeah, this is exactly what I was looking for when I cashed in my 401k and booked this trip. Hey, you with the bone, I don't have all day, let's get this show on the road! Chop chop!

Does your dog bite?

☐ YES ☑ NO

Gnaw, nip, chomp, chew, taste, lick, munch,
nibble, growl, and bark maybe, but never bite.

Would you like a back rub?

 YES ☐ NO

Yes, yes I would.

Would you like a back rub?

☐ YES ☑ NO

Ummmm. I'm good, thanks.

Are you a god?

✅ YES ☐ NO

. . . when someone asks you if you're a god, you say "YES!"

Going somewhere?

 YES ☐ NO

Does this have shellfish in it?

 YES ☐ NO

Oh God. Not good. Listen, I need to get to the hospithull. Thut oh. Thi nee thoo geb thoo tha thospithal! Thut up! Thit's noth foony! Thit's therious!!!

Did you just fart?

☐ YES 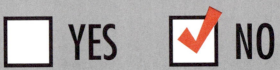 NO

Whaaaa? Noooo. It was probably you! That was not me! I'm insulted, I can't believe you thought I would do that. I don't have to stand here and take this kind of abuse.

(Yeah, it was totally me.)

Would you like a breath mint?

 YES ☐ NO

**It's not a hint. It's a request.
Take three, they're small.**

Are you going to dedicate the book to me?

 YES ☐ NO

I dedicate this book to everyone who has ever asked a question and received nothing but a blank, bewildered stare in return.